G is for Googol

A Math Alphabet Book

Written by David M. Schwartz
Illustrated by Marissa Moss

Tricycle Press
Berkeley, California

Y is for Yael, with love in a googol ways —D.S.

To Dan San Souci —M.M.

Text copyright © 1998 by David M. Schwartz

Illustrations copyright © 1998 by Marissa Moss

TRICYCLE PRESS

P.O. Box 7123

Berkeley, California 94707

www.tenspeed.com

Interior design by Tasha Hall

Cover design by Jean Sanchirico

Library of Congress Cataloging-in-Publication Data

Schwartz, David M.

G is for googol : a math alphabet book / David M. Schwartz;
illustrated by Marissa Moss.

   p. cm.

Summary: Explains the meaning of mathematical terms which
begin with the different letters of the alphabet from abacus, binary,
and cubit to zillion.

ISBN 1-883672-58-9

1. Mathematics—Miscellanea—Juvenile literature.

[1. Mathematics—Miscellanea. 2. Alphabet.]   I. Moss, Marissa, ill.
II. Title.

QA99.S3 61998

510—dc21   98-15162

                                                        CIP

                                                         AC

First printing, 1998

Printed in Singapore

4 5 6 7 8 — 04 03 02 01 00

Contents

Acknowledgments

David Schwartz and Tricycle Press would like to thank the following people for their invaluable participation in the production of this book:

Lisa Crooks, 4th grade teacher, Black Bob Elementary School, Olathe, KS;

Kay Davies, math instructional specialist, Department of Defense Dependent Schools, Japan;

Dr. Ellen Gethner, assistant professor of mathematics, Claremont McKenna College, Claremont, CA;

Barbara Marinak, reading/federal programs coordinator, Central Dauphin School District, Harrisburg, PA;

Laura Norwitz, 6th grade teacher/math coordinator, and all of the student field testers at Rodeph Sholom School, New York, NY: Andrew Gildin, Michael Gunther, Jonah Hecht, Ben Kopelman, Samantha Levine, Adam Marcus, Lauren Roberts, Brian Sander;

Sybil Sevic, curriculum coordinator/math recovery teacher, Ravenel Elementary School, Seneca, SC.

A is for Abacus

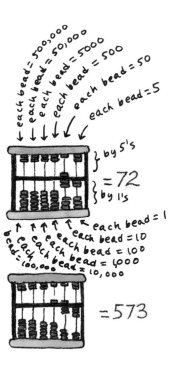

Beads are moved to the middle bar to be counted.

Hundreds of years before calculators were invented, people in China discovered they could add and subtract quickly by sliding beads back and forth on strings. They put seven beads on a string and mounted a few of these strings in a wooden frame. We call the device an *abacus*. It was a great time-saver, and it soon spread to other parts of Asia. The Russians wanted more beads on their abacuses, so they strung ten on each string. The Japanese figured out how to add and subtract just as quickly with only five beads on each string.

Today many people in China and Japan still use abacuses. The strings represent place values (1s, 10s, 100s, etc.), and the positions of the beads along the string represent the number of 1s, 10s, or 100s being used. If you think pushing beads back and forth is slow work, think again. In contests between people using calculators and people using abacuses to add and subtract, the abacus users usually win! Some Chinese and Japanese shopkeepers don't even need a real abacus. They just move their hands in the air, sliding imaginary beads back and forth on imaginary strings. But they still get a real answer!

each bead = 500,000
each bead = 50,000
each bead = 5000
each bead = 500
each bead = 50
each bead = 5

} by 5's
= 72
} by 1's

each bead = 1
each bead = 10
each bead = 100
each bead = 1000
each bead = 10,000
each bead = 100,000

= 573

= 5,255

...and A is also for

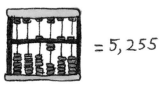

= a happy abacus

acute

algebra

angle

arc

architecture

area

asymmetry

average

axis

Here's the cash for the catch.

Here's the price.

5

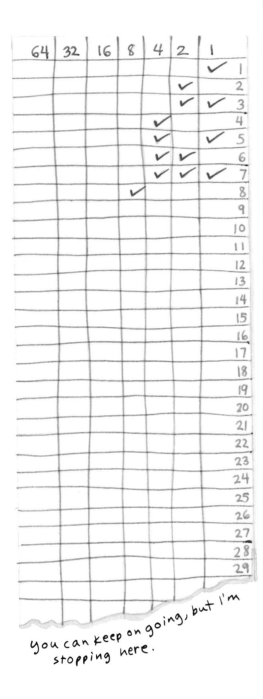

64	32	16	8	4	2	1	
						✔	1
					✔		2
					✔	✔	3
				✔			4
				✔		✔	5
				✔	✔		6
				✔	✔	✔	7
			✔				8
							9
							10
							11
							12
							13
							14
							15
							16
							17
							18
							19
							20
							21
							22
							23
							24
							25
							26
							27
							28
							29

you can keep on going, but I'm stopping here.

...and B is also for

bar graph

base

base number

bisect

B is for Binary

Suppose that instead of getting your regular allowance, you have a choice: You can have a million dollars. Or you can have a penny.

Well, not just a penny, but one cent today, two cents tomorrow, four cents the next day, eight cents the next, and so on, for 30 days. Each day, the amount will double. Which would you choose?

Let's see how many pennies you would get each day during the first week:

1 2 4 8 16 32 64

On the seventh day, you'll receive 64 cents. It doesn't seem like a very good deal, does it? But this is just the first week. While the money is coming in, let's take a close look at the numbers. When you start with 1 and double it to get 2, then double 2 to get 4, then double 4, and keep on doubling, you get a sequence of numbers called the *binary sequence*. The numbers are called binary numbers. There is something very important about *binary numbers*.

You can add binary numbers to make any other number. While 5 is not a binary number, you can make 5 by adding 4 and 1, which are binary numbers. To make 13, add 8, 4, and 1. You can make every number from 1 to 127 out of the first seven binary numbers.

On this page is a chart showing how. On the right side of the chart are decimal numbers—the regular kind you use every day. At the top of the chart are binary numbers. Find the decimal number you want to make and look to the left of it. Wherever you see a check mark, use the binary number at the top of that column. You can create 7 by adding 1, 2, and 4 (that's why they are checked). You can make 13 by adding 8, 4, and 1. We started the chart—now you finish it. *(No, you may not write in the book!)*

Suppose we put a 1 wherever there's a check mark, and a 0 wherever there isn't a check mark. (We won't put anything to the left of the first 1.)

What we have here is the *binary system*, a way of writing numbers using only 1s and 0s. In this system, the number 5 is written 101 and the number 15 is written 1111.

You're probably wondering why anyone would want to write such long, funny-looking numbers with just 1s and 0s that take up so much room on the page. Well, the binary system isn't meant for the page. It's meant for the chip. The computer chip.

Computers "think" in binary. A computer chip has lots and lots of invisible electric switches called bits. A bit can be on or off. That's all it can be. On or off, off or on. It has no brain. It has no variety. It just has on and off. Think of off as the number 0. Think of on as the number 1. Put six bits in a row, and starting at the right side, turn the first one on, turn the next one off, the next one on, the next one off, the next two on. What have you got? You've got the binary number 110101, or 53 in the decimal system. Just use a chart like ours to figure it out.

That's how computers work. A computer turns everything (even letters and pictures and music) into 0s and 1s by turning some bits on and some bits off. The 1s and 0s make binary numbers.

Okay, you say. The binary system can handle small numbers like 1 and 3 and 20 and maybe 153, but it would take billions of bits to make a really big number, like 536,870,912—right? Well, no. It would take only 30 bits to make that number. If you started with 1 and doubled it, then doubled that, and kept doubling, when you got to the 30th number in the binary sequence, you'd have 1000000000000000000000000000000 (a one with 29 zeros). Or in the decimal system, 536,870,912. Exactly.

Remember those pennies? Now we know how many you'd get on the 30th day of doubling: 536,870,912. Hmmm. That's the same as $5,368,709.12. And that doesn't count what you received on each of the other days!

Now which would you choose? A million dollars or a penny?

64	32	16	8	4	2	1	
						1	1
					1	0	2
					1	1	3
				1	0	0	4
				1	0	1	5
				1	1	0	6
				1	1	1	7
			1	0	0	0	8
			1	0	0	1	9
			1	0	1	0	10
			1	0	1	1	11
			1	1	0	0	12
			1	1	0	1	13
			1	1	1	0	14
			1	1	1	1	15
	1	0	0	0	0	0	16
	1	0	0	0	0	1	17
	1	0	0	0	1	0	18
1	0	0	0	0	0	0	64
1	0	0	0	1	0	1	69
1	1	0	0	0	1	1	99
1	1	1	1	1	1	1	127

↖ The torn edges mean numbers are missing – you can fill them in.

↑
With 64¢ you can buy a candy bar — and a gumball, gum from your brother, and some advice— you're rich! (Next week you'll be really wealthy.)

With 1¢ you can buy a penny postage stamp – or someone's thoughts – you know, a penny for your thoughts!

↓

With 2¢ you can get some advice – people are always putting in their 2¢.

↓

With 4¢ you can get a stick of gum from your brother (not already chewed).

↓

With 8¢ you can get your own gumball and have some pennies left.

With 16¢ you can get an eraser from the school book fair and still have a penny.

With 32¢ you can buy a postcard, but you can't afford a stamp, too.

Decipher the secret code. (C is also for code.)

= basket, for K sound

= reed and quail chick, for U sound (as in mule)

= foot, for B sound

= reed, for short or long I sound

= bread for T sound

That's no code - that's hieroglyphs.

= cowbelly - another C word, for the TH sound

C is for Cubit

More than 5,000 years ago, before feet and inches or meters and centimeters were invented, there were *cubits*. In the ancient world, cubits were the common way to measure things. A cubit is the distance from the tip of the elbow to the tip of the middle finger. But there's one little problem: Whose elbow? Whose middle finger?

Suppose you live in ancient Egypt and you pick some papyrus on the banks of the Nile. You take it to the marketplace in Alexandria where you meet Ahmos, a papermaker who has come to shop for papyrus to make his paper.

Ahmos: What lovely papyrus! How much do you want for it?

You: I'll trade 10 cubits of my papyrus for two sheets of your nice paper.

Ahmos: Good deal!

[*You measure out 10 cubits of papyrus and hand it to Ahmos.*]

You: Finally, I can write a letter to my Uncle Ramses.

[*Ahmos gives you the paper, then he checks your measurement on the papyrus.*]

Ahmos: Wait a minute! This isn't 10 cubits. It's only eight cubits. Look!

[*Ahmos shows you that the papyrus is only eight cubits when measured with his forearm.*]

You: Of course it's 10 cubits. Look!!

[*You measure the papyrus again with your own arm.*]

Ahmos: You cheat! You're no better than a thief!! Give me my paper back!!!

You: No, you can't have it. I already wrote "Dear Uncle Ramses" on it. Get outta here!

As you can see, cubits were not the best way to measure things. Nor were the other early units of measure, like digits (a finger's width), palms (four digits), hands (five digits), heads (the height of your head), paces (the length of your step), and so forth. Eventually, people realized that life would be much easier if everyone used the length of the same person's arm (or hand or head). Once they did that, a cubit (or a digit or a pace) was the same for everyone. The exact length that everyone used was a *standard unit* (see **U is for Unit**). Now we have units like centimeters and inches and grams and pounds and degrees and horsepower, and everyone knows what they mean.

But it all started with cubits.

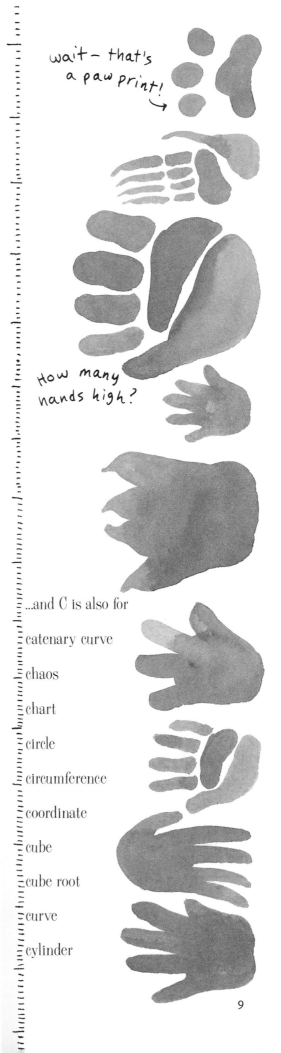

wait— that's a paw print!

How many hands high?

...and C is also for

catenary curve

chaos

chart

circle

circumference

coordinate

cube

cube root

curve

cylinder

D is for Diamond

D iamond shouldn't be in this book. There are diamonds in rings and there are diamonds on baseball fields, but there are no diamonds in math. If you take a square and tilt it on one vertex (corner), it looks like a diamond. But it isn't. It's still a square. If you squeeze it a little so it becomes pointier at two ends and less pointy at the other two ends, it's not a square anymore. But it isn't a diamond, either. It's a *rhombus.*

There are no diamonds in math. We put diamond in this book so you would know it doesn't belong here.

...and D is also for

data

decimal point

decimal system

degree

denominator

density

diameter

dodecahedron

Well, there's no Ace of Squares!

E is for Equilateral

Equi means "equal" and *lateral* means "side," so *equilateral* means "equal sides." When a polygon—a flat shape made from three or more straight sides—has sides that are all equal in length, we say it's equilateral. An equilateral triangle has three sides of the same length. An equilateral pentagon has five sides of the same length. An equilateral hexagon has six sides of the same length.

Big deal. Equilateral is a little boring, so we'll do another **E.**

equilateral circus

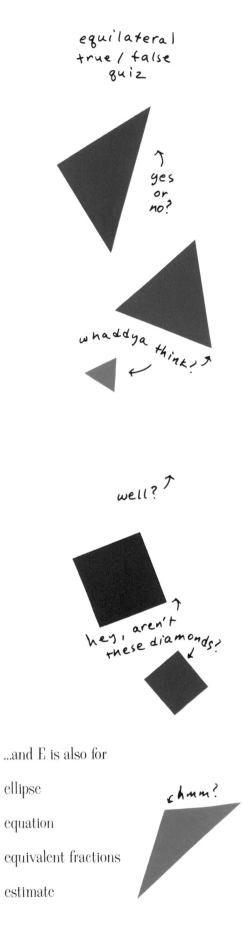

equilateral
true / false
quiz

yes
or
no?

whaddya think!

well?

hey, aren't these diamonds?

...and E is also for

ellipse

equation

equivalent fractions

estimate

ehmm?

E is also for Exponent

E xponents are a little strange at first, but they're definitely not boring. Take a number and multiply it by itself, like this:

$$4 \times 4$$

There's another way to write that:

$$4^2$$

The big 4 at the bottom is called the *base number*, and the little 2 up above is called the *exponent*. The exponent tells you how many times to multiply the base number by itself. So, 4^2 means you multiply two 4s together: 4^2 equals 16. And 4^3 means you multiply three 4s together: 4^3 equals 64. Get it?

2^3 is $2 \times 2 \times 2$. It equals 8.

5^5 is $5 \times 5 \times 5 \times 5 \times 5$, or 3,125.

$7^8 = 7 \times 7 \times 7 \times 7 \times 7 \times 7 \times 7 \times 7 = 5,764,801$

When the base number is 10, something really interesting happens. See if you can figure it out.

$10^6 = 10 \times 10 \times 10 \times 10 \times 10 \times 10 = 1,000,000$ (one million)

$10^9 = 10 \times 10 \times 10 \times 10 \times 10 \times 10 \times 10 \times 10 \times 10 = 1,000,000,000$ (one billion)

2 jelly beans

2 jelly beans to the 2nd power

powerful ↑ jelly beans

2 jelly beans to the 3rd power

may the jelly bean power
be with you!

1 jelly bean

a lonely jelly
bean

1 jelly bean to the 10th power

still 1 lonely jelly bean
(because 1 × 1 × 1 × 1 × 1
× 1 × 1 × 1 × 1 × 1 = $\underline{1}$!)

Did you notice that the number of zeros in the answer is exactly the same as the exponent? That always happens when the base number is 10, so it's really easy to write big numbers with exponents.

Which is easier to write, 10^{12} or 1,000,000,000,000? Now you know why scientists and mathematicians use exponents to write big numbers!

Perhaps you're wondering how a scientist would write a number like two billion. If you're not, please start wondering now.

Here's how:

$$2 \times 10^9$$

2 jelly beans to the 4th power

<u>too</u> many jelly beans to eat in one gulp

now try it with candy corn

or with mints

F is for Fibonacci

In the 1200s, an Italian mathematician named Leonardo of Pisa wrote a book about numbers. He signed his name *Fibonacci* (pronounced fib-o-NOTCH-ee).

In his book, Fibonacci said that the people of Europe should stop using Roman numerals. He wanted everyone to switch to the numerals used in the Arabic world. Instead of writing LXXVIII, they could write 78. Isn't 78 easier to write than LXXVIII? Well, Fibonacci thought so, and because of him, we use Arabic numerals today.

Fibonacci's book also included story problems. One was about rabbits: How many pairs of rabbits will there be each month if you start with one pair of newborn rabbits, and that pair produces a pair of babies every month? The rabbits start producing babies when they are two months old, and their babies also have their first babies when they become two months old.

Here's one way to look at it:

AFTER HOW LONG?	HOW MANY RABBITS?
Starting point	1 pair
After 1 month	1 pair
After 2 months	2 pairs
After 3 months	3 pairs
After 4 months	5 pairs
After 5 months	8 pairs
After 6 months	13 pairs
After 7 months	21 pairs
After 8 months	34 pairs
After 9 months	55 pairs
After 10 months	89 pairs
After 11 months	144 pairs

wow!

Let's look at the answers another way:

$$1 \quad 1 \quad 2 \quad 3 \quad 5 \quad 8 \quad 13 \quad 21 \quad 34 \quad 55 \quad 89 \quad 144$$

These are the first 12 numbers in the famous *Fibonacci sequence* of numbers.

See if you can figure out what's so special about the Fibonacci sequence. After the first two numbers, how can the others be made? Think about it before you read on.

Whenever you add one number to the next, you get the following number in the sequence. Try it. Add 2 and 3. What do you get? Now add 5 and 8. Got it? Okay, now what number comes after 144 in the Fibonacci sequence?

Fibonacci numbers are interesting, but what's *amazing* about them is how often they appear. You can find Fibonacci numbers in art, architecture, music, poetry, and nature. Turn to **N is for Nature.** Get ready to be amazed.

...and F is also for

face

factors

formula

fraction

G is for Googol

A mathematician named Edward Kasner once wrote a 1 followed by 100 zeros. It looked like this:

10,000,000,000,000,000,000,000,000,000,000,000,000,000,
000,000,000,000,000,000,000,000,000,000,000,000,000,000,
000,000,000,000,000

When Kasner wrote this giant number, he asked his nine-year-old nephew, Milton Sirotta, to give it a name. Milton thought for a while, and then he said, "Googol!"

Ever since then, this number has been called a *googol*. You can write it as a 1 with 100 zeros, but there's a much easier way to write a googol. You can use exponents (see **E is for Exponent**):

$$10^{100}$$

Now you can have a googol-writing contest with your friends. See who can write a googol the fastest.

How big is a googol? It's more than the number of grains of sand in the world. It's more than the number of blades of grass in the world. It's more than the number of hairs on the heads of every person in the world. There isn't a googol of anything, anywhere. A googol is more than the number of atoms in the universe. Way more. Would you like to be a googolaire? Where would you put all your money?

Ga ga!

If Kasner had asked his 9-month-old niece, we'd call it a gaga.

...and G is also for

geometry

giga-

golden section (or golden ratio)

gram

graph

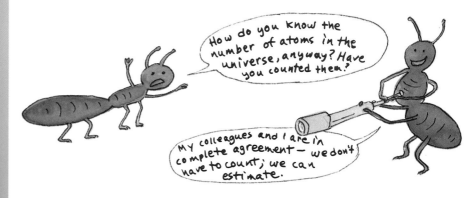

How do you know the number of atoms in the universe, anyway? Have you counted them?

My colleagues and I are in complete agreement— we don't have to count; we can estimate.

G is also for Googolplex

Someone decided that googol wasn't a big enough number, so now we also have *googolplex*. A googolplex is 1 followed by a googol zeros. If you'd like to write that number, go right ahead. We have other things to do.

Well, actually, there is an easy way to write a googolplex. You can use exponents **(see E is for Exponent)**:

$$10^{googol}$$

That means a 1 with a googol zeros—in other words, a googolplex. But maybe you don't like using a word as an exponent. So instead of writing the word *googol* as the exponent, write googol as a number:

$$10^{10,000,000,000,000,000,000,000,000,000,000,000,000,000,000,000,000,000,000,000,000,000,000,000,000,000,000,000,000,000,000,000,000}$$

If that takes too long, here's another way. Since googol can be written 10^{100}, googolplex can be written:

$$10^{10^{100}}$$

The Pied Piper of Zeros

17

How many pence in a pound?

How many pfennigs in a deutsche mark?

How many Europeans in a Euro?

How much money will the people who you send the people who made this book?

...and H is also for

helix

horsepower

hypotenuse

H is for Hundred

Our number system is based on the number 10. Ten 10s are 100. One *hundred* is an important number.

There are 100 cents in a dollar.

In France, there are 100 *centimes* in a *franc*.

In Mexico, there are 100 *centavos* in a *peso*.

There are 100 centimeters in a meter.

In the kind of thermometer used almost everywhere in the world except the United States, there are 100 degrees between freezing and boiling. These are called degrees centigrade or degrees Celsius. Water freezes at 0°C (that's how you write "zero degrees Celsius"), and it boils at 100°C.

There are 100 years in a century. A person who has lived at least 100 years is called a *centenarian*. When a country turns 100 years old, the citizens celebrate the country's *centennial*. One hundred years after that, they celebrate its *bicentennial*.

There are 100 legs on a centipede. Well, not really. There are usually only 30 to 40 legs on a centipede. Whoever named it probably didn't want to get close enough to count its legs, so he guessed it had 100 of them and called it a centipede. Literally, *centipede* means "one hundred feet." There must have been a lot of people who didn't want to get close enough to count the centipede's legs, because the name stuck.

Have you noticed a certain word root that appears over and over again when we're talking about 100? How many times can you find that word root on this page?

what do I have to do with a hundred?

centaur = ?

centimolar = $\frac{1}{100}$ molar

(Dentists use this word all the time — ask a dentist you know today.)

I is for "If"

"If?" you say.
  Yes, "if!"

If is a great word for math problems. Here are a few:

If a million hedgehogs lined up nose-to-tail, nose-to-tail, could they make a prickly necklace around the world? If not, why not?

If you lined up a million tyrannosaurs instead of hedgehogs, would they make it around the world?

If you filled an Olympic-sized swimming pool with ice cream and dived in, how long would it take you to eat your way through the entire pool if you ate ice cream at a rate of one ounce per minute?

If someone gave you a dollar for every math problem you have ever gotten right, how much money would you have? If someone gave you a dollar for every math problem you have ever gotten wrong, would you have even more?

With the word *if*, you can imagine anything and figure out what would happen if it were true. That's one of the things mathematicians and scientists like to do. It helps them make discoveries and understand our world better.

...and I is also for

infinite

infinitessimal

integer

intersection

irrational number

isosceles triangle

J is for Jupiter

Earth is a big place, but *Jupiter* is much bigger. How much bigger? You probably know Jupiter is the largest planet in our solar system, but that doesn't tell you how big it is compared to Earth. Math can help you see the difference.

Let's draw a circle around a button to represent Earth. The diameter of Earth is about 8,000 miles (13,000 kilometers). The diameter of Jupiter is about 88,000 miles (143,000 kilometers). How many times bigger is Jupiter than Earth? To find out, divide the diameter of Jupiter by the diameter of Earth. Jupiter is about 11 times bigger. Now draw Jupiter by making a circle with a diameter that's equal to 11 buttons. Compare the two circles. Do you still think Earth is such a big place?

So does that mean Jupiter is a giant? Let's compare it to the sun.

The sun's diameter is about 880,000 miles (1,430,000 kilometers). How much bigger is the sun than Jupiter? Divide to find out. The sun is about 10 times bigger than Jupiter.

Draw a circle to represent the sun. It should have a diameter of 110 buttons. How can you draw such a big circle? You've probably drawn circles with a compass, but you'll never find a compass large enough to draw this circle! Instead, you could tie a string to a pencil or chalk. Think about how long the string should be. (Answer: 55 buttons.) We can't draw the entire circle representing the sun in this book. It's too big.

This arc shows part of the circle. You can imagine the rest. Hmmm. Jupiter isn't such a giant, after all. But the sun sure is!

our arc ↑

...and J is also for
Jordan curve

Or is it? What if we compared the sun to something even bigger—like Betelgeuse, a star of the type called a *red giant*. You can draw a circle to show Betelgeuse compared to the sun. All you need to know is that Betelgeuse is about 792,000,000 miles (1,275,000,000 kilometers) in diameter.

Figure out how many times bigger than the sun it is. Maybe you can draw a circle to show Betelgeuse compared to Earth, Jupiter, and the sun. You'll need a long string, a thick piece of chalk...and a really big playground!

Is there such a thing as "big"? Is there such a thing as "small"?

Does it surprise you that math can help us learn something about science? Math is a tool used to understand the world around us, so scientists use math all the time. If you want to be a scientist, you're going to use math. Lots of math.

K is for Königsberg

Once there was a city in Germany called *Königsberg*. The Pregel River ran through the center of the city. In the 1700s, seven bridges connected two islands in the river to the rest of the city. The people of Königsberg liked to stroll around the city on Sundays. For fun, they tried to find a way to cross all seven bridges without crossing any bridge more than once. Can you find a route that crosses each bridge only once?

Don't worry if you can't. The people of Königsberg couldn't either. But the "Königsberg bridge problem" became famous all over Europe. No one could understand why it was impossible to walk all the bridges, crossing each one only once, until a Swiss mathematician named Leonhard Euler (pronounced OIL-er) invented a new kind of math called *network theory*. A network is a crisscrossing web of lines, which is what you get on the page when you try to solve the Königsberg bridge problem with a pencil! Some people call networks "the mathematics of wiggly lines."

Euler figured out which kinds of networks can be walked without retracing any steps, and which cannot. He proved that it was impossible to walk a route that crossed each of the Königsberg bridges only once, no matter how you did it.

But don't let that stop you from trying. Have a nice walk!

Pregel River

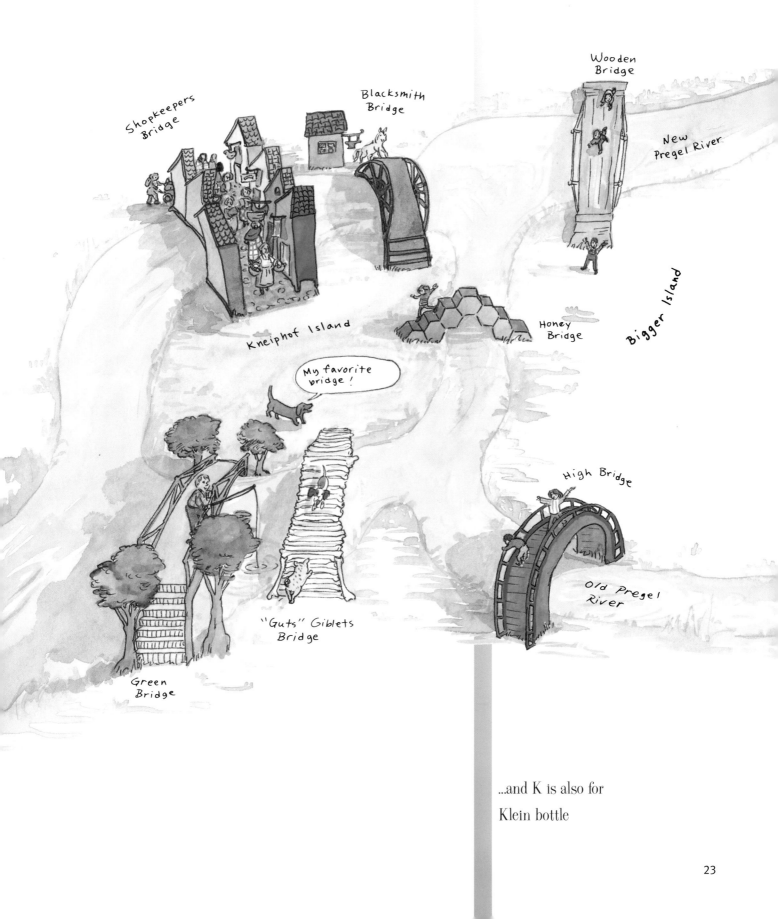

← this is _not_ a bridge

Wooden Bridge

New Pregel River

Shopkeepers Bridge

Blacksmith Bridge

Bigger Island

Kneiphof Island

Honey Bridge

My favorite bridge!

High Bridge

"Guts" Giblets Bridge

Old Pregel River

Green Bridge

...and K is also for
Klein bottle

L is for Light-Year

Does a *light-year* sound like a very short year? Or a year when you don't eat a lot? Actually, it's neither. In fact, a light-year isn't light, and it's not a kind of year, either! It's a standard unit (see **C is for Cubit** and **U is for Unit**) used to measure distances. BIG distances! Astronomers usually use light-years to measure distances in space.

A light-year is the distance light travels in a year. The closest star to our solar system, Proxima Centauri (one star in a three-star system called Alpha Centauri) is about four light-years away. When you look at Proxima Centauri, you're actually looking at light that left the star more than four years ago. If Proxima Centauri burned out three years ago, we wouldn't find out about it for another year!

Traveling at a speed of one mile per second, a spaceship would reach Proxima Centauri in about 800,000 years. In a car it would take you…oh, roughly 50 million years—depending on how fast you drive, of course. Now, don't forget that Proxima Centauri is the *closest* star to our solar system, not the farthest. Some stars are millions, even billions, of light-years away.

So just how many miles (or kilometers) are in a light-year? To figure it out, we need to know that the speed of light is 186,282 miles (299,784 kilometers) per second. This distance is more than seven times around the Earth.

4.2 light years to Earth

Proxima Centauri

That means that in one second, light travels so far that it could go around the Earth more than seven times—if it went in circles (which it doesn't). Snap your fingers. One second just went by, and light from the stars just traveled a distance of more than seven times around the Earth. Mind-boggling, isn't it? But we still haven't told you how far light travels in a year.

To do the math, multiply the speed of light by 60 to find out how many miles it travels in a minute, then multiply that by 60 to find out how many miles it travels in an hour, and keep going until you get to years (remember to use $365\frac{1}{4}$ or 365.25 days in a year.) So, there are 5,878,512,843,200 miles or 9,460,463,558,400 kilometers in a light-year. Can you see why astronomers use light-years?

It's been 4 years—that light should be here any month now.

We're waaaiting!

Are we there yet?

CAUTION
BLACK HOLE
12 Light-Years Away

Galaxy Gifts

NO PARKING 9-5 except Sat. and Sun.

...and L is also for

latitude

line graph

locus

logic

longitude

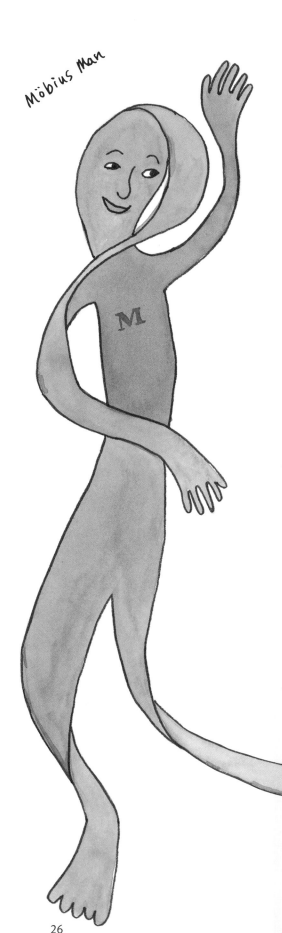

Möbius Man

M is for Möbius Strip

Take a strip of paper and tape one end to the other to make it into a loop. Let's call it a "belt loop."

Now make another loop with another strip of paper, but this time give the strip a twist before you tape the two ends together. You wouldn't call this a belt loop unless you accidentally twist your belt every time you put it on. This kind of loop is a *Möbius strip*.

A Möbius strip is a mathematical wonder.

The ordinary belt loop has two sides—an inside and an outside. If you wanted to, you could paint just one side. Go ahead, paint one side of your belt loop. Easy. One side is painted, and the other side is blank.

Now try to paint just one side of the Möbius strip. Good luck!

My side!

No, my side!

Topologists are mathematicians who study what happens to various shapes and solids when they are pushed and pulled and twisted and cut and contorted in different ways. A topologist would say that a Möbius strip has only one side. Can that be? What happened when you tried to paint just one side of your Möbius strip? Where is the other side? If there is no "other" side, then the Möbius strip must have only one side.

What good is a Möbius strip? Aside from being fun, Möbius strips are actually useful. In factories, conveyor belts are often made like Möbius strips. If they were made like regular belts, one side would wear out quickly. When made like a Möbius strip, the whole belt lasts twice as long.

Here's another strange thing about the Möbius strip. Run a pencil line all the way down its center. What do you think will happen if you cut along the pencil line with scissors? Try it. Draw a pencil line down the center of the new strip. Predict what will happen if you cut along this line, then do it.

Make another Möbius strip, but don't draw a pencil line down the center. Instead, draw it one-third of the way in from one edge. What do you predict will happen if you cut along this line? Do it. Are you surprised? Everyone else is, too—except topologists, of course.

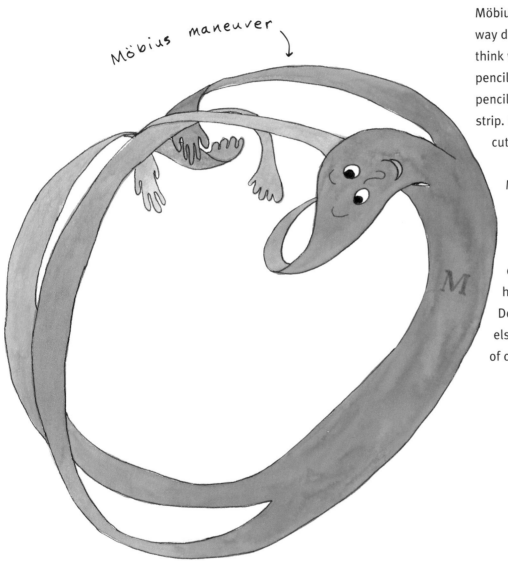

Möbius maneuver

M

...and M is also for

mankala

mass

mean, median, and mode

metric system

N is for Nature

There are numbers in *nature*. Lots.

Do you remember the Fibonacci sequence of numbers? (See **F is for Fibonacci.**) Here are the first twelve numbers of the Fibonacci sequence:

1 1 2 3 5 8 13 21 34 55 89 144

Fibonacci discovered this number sequence, but he did not invent it. Nature invented it. If each page of this book stated one way that Fibonacci numbers appear in nature, we'd need a book so heavy you couldn't lift it. Here are just a few.

The number of petals in a flower is usually a Fibonacci number. Some flowers, like daisies, don't have true petals, but petal-like parts called *florets*. Florets come in Fibonacci numbers, too.

Three kinds of spirals in a pineapple

Pine needles come in groups, or *bundles*. The bundles almost always have 1, 2, 3, or 5 needles. Do these numbers look familiar?

But pine needles aren't nearly as interesting as pinecones. Find a pinecone. The hard little knubby parts are called *bracts*. (Make sure your pinecone is in good condition, with no missing bracts.) Turn the cone so you're looking at its base. Can you see how the bracts make spirals? There are clockwise spirals, and there are counterclockwise spirals. Follow one spiral as it winds all the way around the cone to the pointy end. Dab a little paint on each bract in that spiral. Now dab a different color on a spiral going in the other direction. You'll see that one spiral winds gradually, and the other one winds more steeply. How many of each type are there? Count them. Remember, it's not the number of bracts that you're counting; it's the number of spirals.

spirals one way are checkerboard

spirals the other way are red and yellow lines

bottom of a pinecone

Some pinecones have 3 gradual spirals and 5 steep spirals. Some have 5 gradual and 8 steep. Or 8 and 13. Or 13 and 21. A pinecone's spirals come in Fibonacci numbers. In fact, Fibonacci numbers are sometimes called "pinecone numbers."

Fibonacci numbers could also be called "sunflower numbers," "artichoke numbers," or "pineapple numbers" because you will find the numbers in spirals formed by a sunflower's seeds, an artichoke's leaves, and a pineapple's scales (the diamond-shaped markings on the outside).

Fibonacci strikes again!

first rectangle

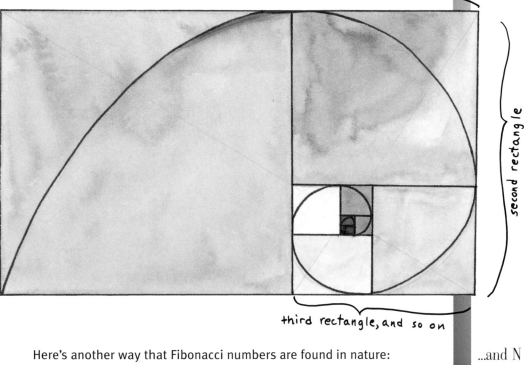

second rectangle

third rectangle, and so on

No one really understands why Fibonacci numbers show up so much in nature. It's a mystery!

Here's another way that Fibonacci numbers are found in nature: They make a spiral that maintains a constant proportion all the way to infinity. To find that spiral, take a rectangle that has "Fibonacci" proportions, say 3" x 5", then repeat that same proportioned rectangle, smaller and smaller...

...and N is also for

negative number

nim

numerator

O is for Obtuse

25°

57°

110°

150°

Put your hands together, palm-to-palm, in front of your face. Now move them apart just a teenie bit, except at the base of the palms. We can think of your hands as line segments. The two lines come together at the base where they're touching. Where two lines come together, they make an opening called an *angle*. Right now, the angle between your hands is very small. Keep the base of your palms together and slowly move your hands apart so there is more space between them. The angle is getting bigger.

As you see, angles come in different sizes. Mathematicians use a unit called a *degree* to measure them. (See **U is for Unit.**) A very small angle might be 5 degrees or 10 degrees, usually written 5° or 10°. (The little circle is the symbol for degrees, just as in temperature, but we're not talking about how hot or cold your hands are.) Open your hands a little more, and keep going until your hands look like this:

Help! I'm caught in the Bermuda Triangle!

right angle

oooh — what acute angle, just darling!

leg angle (angle — ankle, get it?)

This is an important angle. So important that it has two names: it's called a *90° angle* and a *right angle*. (Not that there are any wrong angles.) You can find four right angles in every square and every rectangle. A triangle could have one right angle, or it might not have any. (But it certainly can't have more than one.) Triangles with a right angle are called *right triangles*. Unless you live in a cave or a very unusual building, your home has right angles between the walls and between the walls and the floor. In most houses, there are also right angles between the walls and the ceiling.

Okay, break time. Shake out your hands. Better yet, make some hand shadows.

That's enough fooling around with shadows. Time to go back to fooling around with angles. Start again with your hands pressed together (you could say they have a 0° angle between them if they're completely touching) and increase the angle size until it reaches 90°, just as before. All of the angles you have just made are less than 90°. They're called *acute angles*. (No, not "cute angles," no matter how good-looking they are. *Acute angles*.)

This time, don't stop at 90°. Separate the tips of your fingers some more. Now the angles are bigger than 90°. Here's 120°… and 150° and… can you stretch all the way… until your hands… are directly opposite each other? We can't, but maybe you can. If so, your hands now make one continuous line. The measurement between them is 180°.

Angles between 90° and 180° are called *obtuse angles*. See if you can find acute, right, and obtuse angles in these pictures.

...and O is also for

octave

oware

P is for Probability

You've probably heard weather reports that go something like this: "Bad news, folks. There's a 90 percent chance of rain tomorrow."

What does that mean? A "100 percent chance" would mean that rain is absolutely certain tomorrow. Ninety percent is almost 100 percent, so rain is not certain tomorrow, but it's very likely. When you hear the bad news, you cancel your plans for a picnic.

Tomorrow comes, and it's a beautiful sunny day.

Probability is the mathematics of predictions. Predicting is not the same as guessing, but predictions, like guesses, can be wrong. Predictions are based on information, or *data*, that is definite, combined with other information that is uncertain. A "90 percent chance of rain" means that 9 times out of 10, it rained on a day like today. That's a probability of 90 percent. That's all weather forecasters can tell you. Remember—on one day out of 10 days like today, the sun shone. That's why weather forecasters make no promises. But go ahead. Blame the weather on them. They're used to it.

Weather forecasters aren't the only ones who use probability. Cardplayers and other gamblers know certain facts about cards or dice, and those facts help them decide how to bet. They are using probability. Doctors use probability when they give you medicine. They don't know for sure that the medicine will make you well, but they know how it works for a lot of other people so they can predict how likely it is to help you. Your mother uses probability when she says, "Eat your broccoli!" Broccoli will probably help you grow up healthy, but once in a rare while, it might make you sick. (Try that one on your mother!)

If you're a sports fan and you've ever said something like "I'll betcha the Texas Tomatoes wipe out the Michigan Mushrooms in the Veggie Bowl," you were using probability. If you know that the Tomatoes have already won 14 out of 15 games this year, while the Mushrooms have won only 1, then the Tomatoes are a good bet to win. But they could have a really bad day.

The probability of me ordering pizza for lunch is 100%!

The more you study probability, the more you realize there's no such thing as "a sure thing." There are only probabilities—high, low, and in between. The mathematics of probability helps you figure out how high, how low, or where in between. What do you think the chances are that your mother will notice you stuffing that broccoli in your pocket?

Of the 10 vegetables in the refrigerator, what is the probability of being served broccoli for dinner?

who put this broccoli here? Probably it was you!

...and P is also for

palindrome

parabola

parallel

parallelogram

percent

pi

pie chart

point

polygon

polyhedron

prime number

proportion

Pythagorean theorem

Is this just a run of bad luck or highly improbable?

THURSDAY

I bet this is that same smelly broccoli.

4 days in a row: 1 in 10,000

FRIDAY

It was gross yesterday, the day before yesterday, the day before that, and the day before that — it's definitely disgusting!

5 days in a row: 1 in 100,000

SATURDAY

If I see broccoli one more time, I'm NEVER coming to the table again!

6 days in a row: 1 in a million

P is for Probability

Based on data we've collected from thousands of readers like you, there's a very high probability that you thought we were done with probability. But we're not. We're doing **P is for Probability** again so you can actually collect data and calculate probabilities.

First, you need to know that there are several different ways to state a probability. One is the way the weather forecasters do it on TV. They give a percentage. A 50 percent chance of rain means there are 50 chances out of 100 that it will rain. You can also state probability as a fraction. Fifty percent is the same as $\frac{50}{100}$ or $\frac{1}{2}$. Those are two ways to give probabilities—percentages and fractions. There are others, but that's enough for now.

When you flip a coin, there are two ways it can come up: heads or tails. These two ways are called *outcomes*. With coins, the two possible outcomes are equally likely, so there's one chance out of two that you'll flip heads, and one chance out of two that you'll flip tails. Instead of saying "one out of two," you can say that the chance of flipping a coin and getting heads is one-half. (The chance of getting tails is also one-half, of course.)

Try it. Flip a coin twice. Did you get heads once and tails once? Maybe you did, maybe you didn't. Probability doesn't tell you what the outcome will be. It just tells you what it's likely to be, and how likely that is. You flipped the coin two times. That's not much. To test predictions, you need a lot of data. Flip the coin 10 times and keep track of the outcomes. Did you get heads half the time and tails half the time? You can chart your results on a bar graph like this.

Even 10 coin flips aren't very many. Flip the coin 20 times. Are your results any

Heads   Tails

closer to being even-steven? Go for 50 flips. Try 100. How close are you now to getting half heads and half tails? Graph the outcomes and see. Do you think you'd be closer still if you flipped the coin 1,000 times? The more data you have, the more accurately you can state a probability. Is the probability of getting heads when you flip a coin really one-half (or 50 percent)?

It's inconvenient to collect data when you want to know a probability. Once again, math comes to the rescue! We can use math to figure out the chance of flipping heads twice in a row (or three times, or four times, etc.)

When mathematicians talk about flipping coins, they describe flips as *independent events* because flipping heads the first time has no effect on what you'll flip the second time. When you want to know the probability of two independent events occurring together, you multiply the probabilities of their happening separately. The chance of flipping tails once is one-half and the chance of flipping tails a second time is also one-half. But the chance of flipping tails *both* times is $\frac{1}{2}$ x $\frac{1}{2}$, or $\frac{1}{4}$. (If you don't know how to multiply fractions, don't worry. Instead of saying "one-half *times* one-half," say "one-half *of* one-half." Then it's easy to see that the answer is one-fourth. Try multiplying other fractions this way until you get a feel for it.)

Now that you know something about the mathematics of probability, can you figure the chance of flipping tails three times in a row? It would be $\frac{1}{2}$ x $\frac{1}{2}$ x $\frac{1}{2}$, or $\frac{1}{8}$. How about four heads? Ten tails? You would be mighty lucky to flip 10 tails in a row, and we think there's a good chance you can now figure out the chance (or *odds*) of doing it.

Now try flipping two coins, say a penny and a nickel. What do you think the probability is that you'll get two heads? To make this prediction, you need to know how many possible outcomes there are. Both coins can come up heads. Call that HH.

The penny can come up heads, and the nickel can come up tails: HT.

The penny can come up tails and the nickel can come up heads: TH.

Both coins can come up tails: TT.

There are four outcomes, and only one of those four is HH, so you might predict that the probability of both coins coming up heads is one in four, or one-fourth. What is the probability of flipping two tails? One head and one tail? Test it out. Flip your two coins and keep track of the outcomes. Remember to get lots of data. Graph your results. Do your data agree with your prediction?

Q is for Quantity
—and Quality

In math, we often add, subtract, multiply, and do other things to numbers. In the end, we get another number for an answer. It tells us "how many" or "how much." It tells us a *quantity*. But if you know only quantity, you don't know enough.

Someone offers you a million. Do you take it? If it's dollars, sure! "Back up the truck right here!" you say. But it could be a million pounds of cooked octopus. Or a million wedges of stinky cheese. Or a million pages of math worksheets. You might be happy to have a kitten. Or a sister. Or a few kittens or sisters. But would you really want a million of them?

When we talk about "what," we're talking about *quality*. You'd better know the qualities of something—its features, its characteristics, its identity—before you take a million. Quality also means how good something is. Would you like a million dollars? Not if it's play money. That's not the quality you had in mind. How about a million pizzas? You'd better be sure they're not cold and soggy or topped with liver and brussels sprouts.

In many math problems, quantity may be all that you need to know. But in life, you'd better know both the quantity *and* the quality, or you might end up with 500 bushels—of cockroaches!

Pssst— have I got a deal for you. You give me $20, and I give <u>you</u> a million!

A million bunches of BROCCOLI!

NO!

...and Q is also for

quadrilateral

quipu

R is for
Rhombicosidodecahedron

"Excuse me?"

Rhombicosidodecahedron. (ROM-bi-cosi-DOE-DECK-a-HEE-dron.) Say it a few times, and it'll roll right off your tongue. You can impress your parents and your friends. You can say things like "Do you happen to have a rhombicosidodecahedron I can borrow?"

Now that you can pronounce it, perhaps you'd like to know what it is. A rhombicosidodecahedron is a special kind of *polyhedron*.

"What kind of polyhedron?" you say. "And what's a polyhedron, anyway?"

A polyhedron is a three-dimensional shape with flat sides. The flat sides are also called *faces*. A cube is a very simple polyhedron. It has six sides, or faces. All of them are squares. Tetrahedrons have four faces, all triangles. Octahedrons have eight faces (all triangles), dodecahedrons have 12 faces (all hexagons), and icosahedrons have 20 faces (all triangles). A rhombicuboctahedron has 26 faces. Eighteen of them are squares and eight are triangles. There are plenty of other polyhedrons, but the biggest one we know is the rhombicosidodecahedron. It has 240 faces! And they're all triangles.

Leonhard Euler, the mathematician who worked on the Königsberg bridge problem (see **K is for Königsberg**), also discovered something no one had ever noticed before about polyhedrons. He looked at the number of faces, the number of edges (the lines where faces meet), and the number of vertices (the points where edges meet). No matter what kind of polyhedron Euler looked at, the number of vertices plus the number of sides always equalled the number of edges plus 2. To write it in a mathematical way, he used the letter e for the number of edges, the letter v for the number of vertices, and the letter s for the number of sides. Then he wrote the equation that is now called *Euler's formula:*

$$v + s = e + 2$$

...and R is also for

radius

ratio

rhombus

right angle

right triangle

rotational symmetry

Take a cube

Count the sides (or faces)

Count the vertices (or corners)

Count the edges

That may seem scary, but it isn't. It just says that the number of vertices (*v*) plus the number of sides (*s*) equals the number of edges (*e*) plus 2. Try it out with a cube. In a cube there are 8 vertices (*v*), 6 sides (*s*) and 12 edges (*e*). So, just plug those numbers into Euler's formula:

$$8 + 6 = 12 + 2$$

Is it true? Does 8 + 6 equal 12 + 2? They both add up to 14, so Euler's formula works for a cube.

Try Euler's formula for some other polyhedrons. Then try it for a rhombicosidodecahedron. You probably won't be able to borrow one, so we'll tell you a few things about it. It has 240 sides and 122 vertices. You want to know how many edges? We're not going to tell you because you can figure it out for yourself by using Euler's formula.

Or make yourself a rhombicosidodecahedron and count the edges.

Everyone knows a rhombicosidodecahedron is a rhino with the swine flu— achoo!

hey – a tissue box is a polyhedron!

S is for Symmetry

Meet Sam. Can you draw a line dividing her face into two mirror images? If you held a little mirror on that line, or folded the picture along that line, the two halves would match perfectly. We call the line a *line of symmetry*, and we say that Sam's face has *symmetry*. Or that it is *symmetrical*. Symmetry gives beauty and balance to the world around us.

Meet Starr, a starfish. Is Starr symmetrical? Sam was symmetrical in just one way because she had just one line of symmetry, but you should be able to find more than one line of symmetry in Starr. How many? How many lines of symmetry are in a snowflake? A maple leaf? A microscopic sea urchin larva?

A square is simpler than a snowflake or a sea urchin larva, but that doesn't mean finding its lines of symmetry is simple. Can you find four? Don't quit until you do. How many can you find in the capital letter H? In E? In these flags? In the other shapes?

Is there symmetry in a hot dog?

In a piece of pizza?

A thing of symmetry is a joy forever (or, in the case of pizza, is tasty when fresh).

Aren't I beautiful?

...and S is also for

scalene

sequence

set

SI unit

sphere

spiral

square

square root

Meet Cirque. Cirque is a plain old circle. We just felt like giving it a fancy name. Is Cirque symmetrical? How many lines of symmetry does Cirque have? We don't want you to spend the rest of your life counting them, so we'll tell you right now that Cirque has infinite lines of symmetry. All circles do. No matter how close you draw the lines of symmetry, you can always stick in more (if you have a thin enough pencil). Do you think anything besides a circle is symmetrical in an infinite number of ways? The answer is no. Only a circle is infinitely symmetrical.

Meet sPin. sPin is a pinwheel. You cannot find any lines of symmetry in the pinwheel. It doesn't have *line symmetry* (also called *mirror symmetry*). But a pinwheel is symmetrical. If you rotate it one-half of a turn, it looks exactly like it did before. It has *rotational symmetry* (or *point symmetry*).

How about the tire? Is it infinitely symmetrical? with Hub or without?

Here is Hub. Hub is a hubcap. It has both rotational symmetry and line symmetry. Can you see why?

Some objects have rotational symmetry, some have line symmetry, some have neither, and some have both.

Take a closer look at Sam. Is she truly symmetrical? Are you? Is anything in nature perfectly symmetrical?

Hint: the nose knows.

T is for Tessellate

Bees haven't read this book, but they know how to tessellate. They make cells of wax that completely cover the walls of their hive. Each cell is a hexagon, and all the hexagons fit together perfectly. When shapes cover a surface with no gaps in between, we say the shapes *tessellate*.

Look at these five shapes. They are *regular polygons*. In a regular polygon, all of the sides are the same length, and all of the angles are also the same.

Only three of these regular polygons tessellate. Which ones? Find some regular polygons (or make them from paper or cardboard) and spread them out on the table or floor. Try to fit them together. Tessellate away!

Sometimes you have to use two kinds of shapes to tessellate a surface. You can't tessellate with octagons alone, but you can tessellate if you add another shape. What is it? Many bathroom floors are covered with tiles like these. Which two shapes tessellate on the surface of a soccer ball? (If they didn't tessellate, the ball would go flat in no time!)

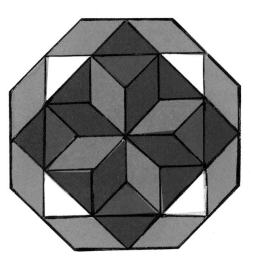

Irregular shapes can also tessellate. For centuries, Islamic artists have created tessellating patterns to cover floors, walls, ceilings, and doors. A Dutch artist named M. C. Escher became famous for his strange prints of tessellating creatures—birds, fish, other animals, even knights on horseback!

But back to those bees. They tessellate hexagons to make their honeycomb. Why don't they use triangles or squares or a combination of different shapes? The answer is very interesting.

Of the three tessellating regular polygons, hexagons have the smallest perimeter (that's the distance around the outside) compared to their area (that's the amount of space inside). This makes hexagons a good deal for the bees. It's sort of like shopping. You want to get the best game or shirt or pizza for the

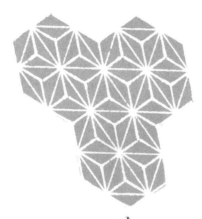

...and T is also for

table

tangram

topology

triangle

triskaidekaphobia

41

amount of money you spend. Bees want to get the most space to store honey for the least amount of wax they have to "spend" to build their honeycomb. With just 1.48 ounces (42 grams) of wax laid down in hexagons, worker bees can build a honeycomb that holds more than 5 pounds (2 kilograms) of honey! If they used any other shape, the bees would have to use more wax to hold the same amount of honey.

It pays to be good at math—even if you're a bee.

How do bees make these shapes so well? It's hard enough to draw them— you try it!

U is for Unit

1 foot foot ↗

½ foot foot ↗

ᴮack when people used cubits and hands and strides to measure lengths of things (see **C is for Cubit**), they eventually realized that it worked best when one person set the standard. Usually that person was the king. In Egypt about 5,000 years ago, the distance from the pharaoh's elbow to the tip of his middle finger became the first standard unit of length. It was called the *royal cubit*. Nowadays, we would call it 20.6 inches, or 52.3 centimeters.

Of course, the pharaoh was too busy to take his elbow all over the place just so everyone else could measure papyrus. Instead, lines were scratched in a piece of wood or metal to show the size of the royal cubit. TA-DAH! The first ruler. Actually, it was called a *measuring stick*. The beauty of a measuring stick was that it could be used to make other measuring sticks. The pharaoh could stay home and eat grapes or take bubble baths, or do whatever pharaohs did in their spare time.

Standard units of measure were a big improvement over everyone using his or her own body parts, but there was still a problem. It was impossible to get all of the measuring sticks to be *exactly* the same. Today's standard units of length are based on waves of laser light. Laser light waves do not change, whether it's summer or winter, Alaska or Arabia. For most people most of the time, any wooden or metal ruler works just fine, but your ruler and your friend's ruler might be slightly different. Probably it won't matter, but if you need a highly accurate measurement because you've just invented a new kind of computer chip that you plan to manufacture in your garage, the differences from one ruler to another could be important. And with changes in the weather, some rulers might shrink or lengthen a little bit.

There are also standard units of weight, volume, time, temperature, power, energy, and everything else people want to measure. We still use some of the old words, like *horsepower*, but the standard unit itself is the same everywhere, no matter how strong or weak (or dead) your own horse happens to be.

⌐and here's the royal foot (er, feet)

...and U is also for

union

V is for Venn Diagram

When you got to school last Monday, Ms. Mathemacallit took the roll in a peculiar way. She asked everyone to sign a chart in the appropriate place.

Some wise guy signed Hubert in a strange place. Why?

MONDAY

On Tuesday, Ms. Mathemacallit put out another odd chart. It was similar to the one on Monday, but it had some differences.

Why did some people sign this chart in the overlapping areas, while others did not? What is Grace wearing under her sandals? What could Elizabeth be wearing under hers? What could Erica B., Khasha, and Dianne be wearing over their socks? And why do you suppose no one signed in the bottom part of the lowest circle?

These kinds of charts are called *Venn diagrams*. They are easy to make and easy to read, and you can learn a lot from them in just one glance. What you see inside each circle is called a *set*. You could say, "Amanda is in the set of people who are wearing sandals." The *intersection* where two sets overlap shows the people who belong in *both* categories. Richard is in the set of people who are wearing sandals *and* socks.

On Wednesday, Ms. M. had another Venn diagram. This one was really strange.

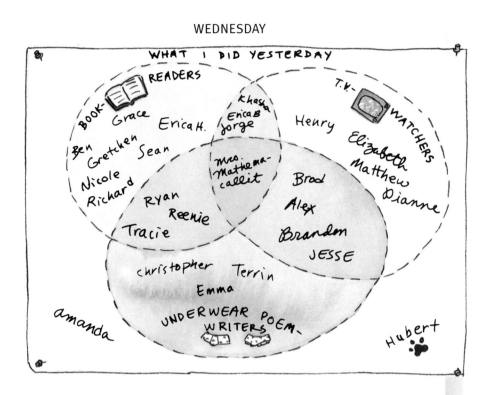

Can you tell how many people read *G is for Googol* (or some other book)? Make sure you include the people who read but also did other things. How many people watched TV? Who wrote poems about underwear and also read a book? How many underwear poets also watched TV?

You can find out who watched TV *and* wrote an underwear poem by looking for the place where the set of couch potatoes *intersects* the set of underwear poets. But what about the people who watched TV *or* wrote an underwear poem? Can the Venn diagram help us find them? Sure, we just have to look at both sets together. This is called the *union* of the two sets. The intersection of two sets is the area where they overlap; the union of the two sets is the entire area of one set plus the entire area of the other. Jesse, Brad, Ms. M., Alex (and many others) are in the union of the two sets (couch potatoes and underwear poets). That means they watched TV or they wrote an underwear poem or they did both. But Grace, Gretchen, Ben, Erica H., Sean, Nicole, Richard, and Amanda did neither. In the Venn diagram, they are not in the union of those two sets.

Why do you think Amanda (and Hubert) are outside all three circles?

...and V is also for

variable

vertex

volume

On Thursday, Ms. M. had yet another chart. This one was *really* different.

None of these circles overlap the way they did on Tuesday or Wednesday. Instead, the smaller circles are completely inside the larger ones, like a target. Where do you think the school is located? Can you come up with a reason why Reenie and Erica B. are not in the center circle along with everyone else? And hooray for Hubert! He finally made it inside a circle. How come?

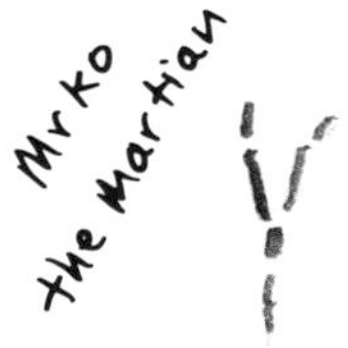

HOME SWEET HOME

I LIVE ON EARTH

I LIVE IN THE U.S.A.

I LIVE IN LOUISIANA

I LIVE IN NEW ORLEANS

Erica B.

Ryan
Jorge
Khasha   Richard   Jean   Brandon
Christopher   Elizabeth   Erica H.
Henry   Brod
Tracie   Hubert   Matthew
Ben   JESSE
Emma   Terrin   Grace   Dianne   Reenie
Amanda   Alex   Nicole   Gretchen

46

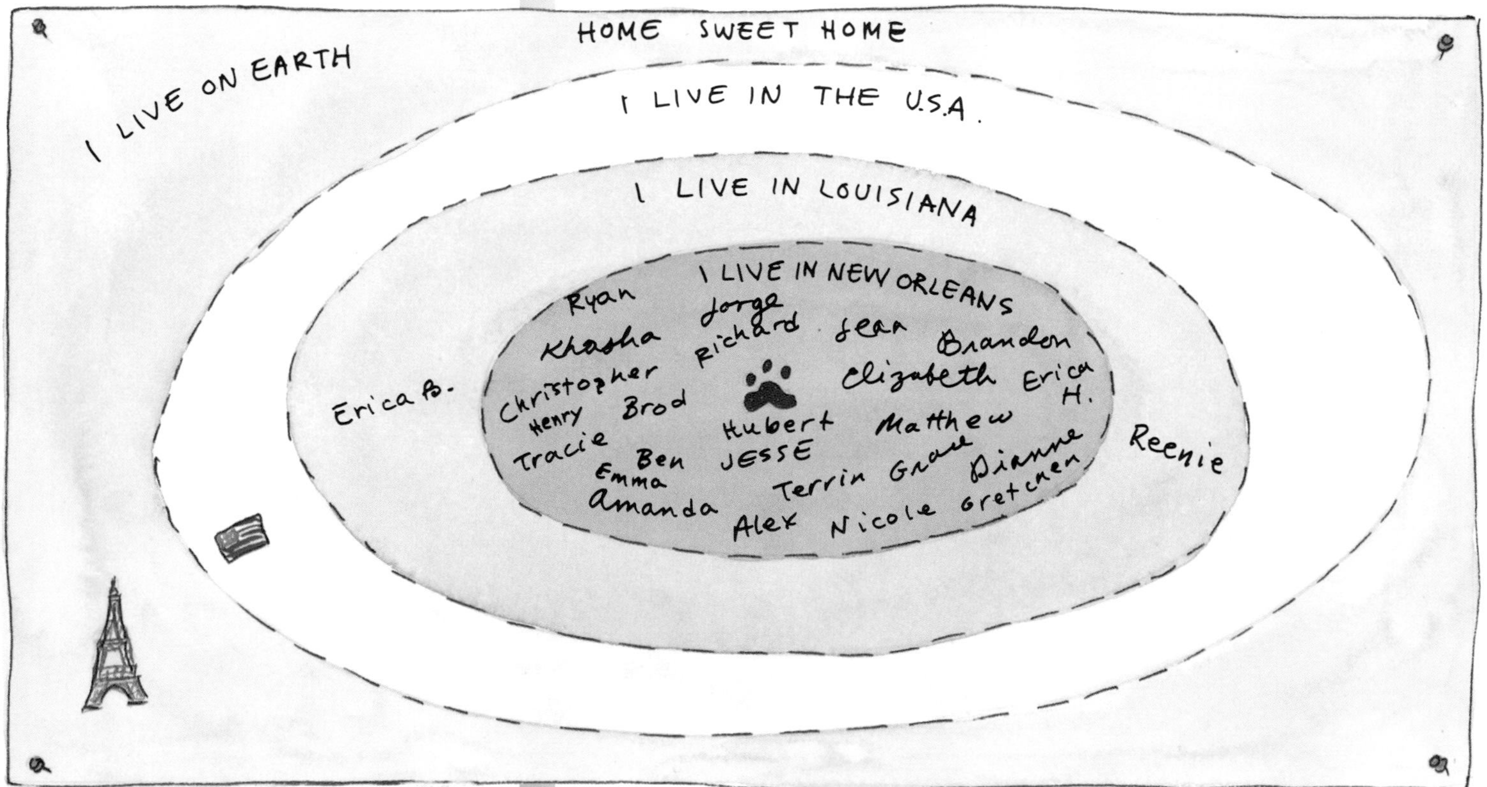

Venn diagrams don't have to be made with circles. Any shape might do. And Venn diagrams don't have to be about people. Think about other foods that could go in this Venn diagram. Then think of some wild and wacky Venn diagrams that you could make for your class to sign.

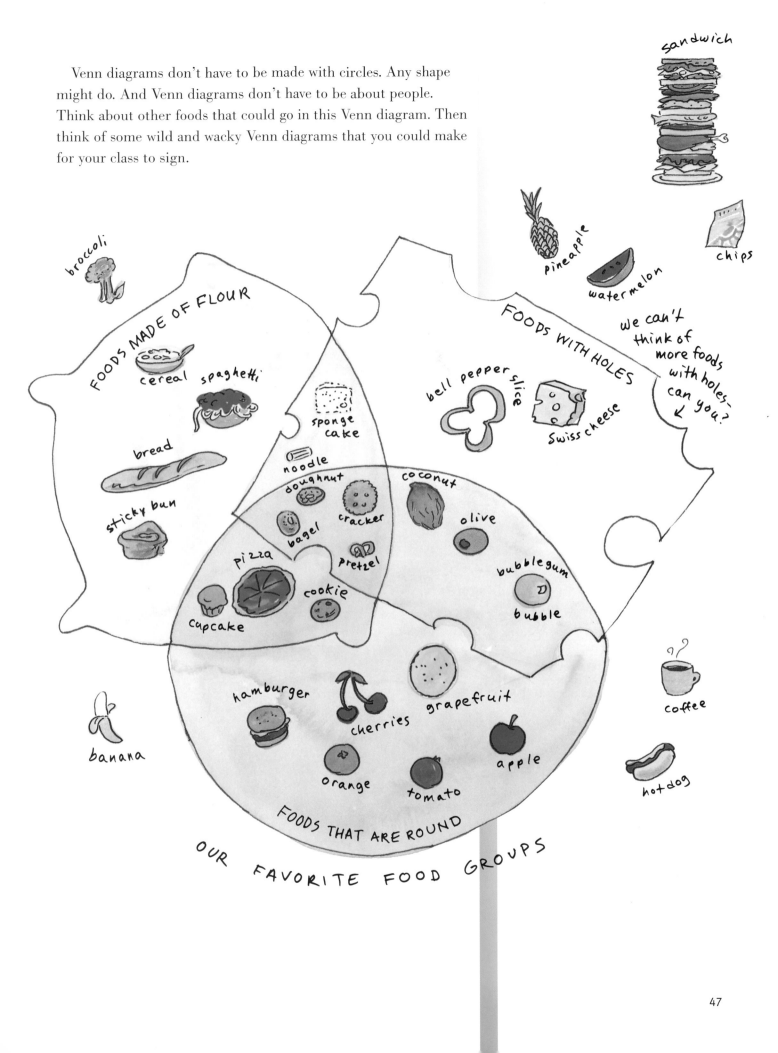

sandwich

pineapple

watermelon

chips

broccoli

FOODS MADE OF FLOUR

cereal

spaghetti

sponge cake

FOODS WITH HOLES

bell pepper slice

Swiss cheese

we can't think of more foods with holes— can you?

bread

noodle

doughnut

coconut

sticky bun

bagel

cracker

olive

pizza

pretzel

bubble gum

cupcake

cookie

bubble

banana

hamburger

cherries

grapefruit

coffee

orange

tomato

apple

hot dog

FOODS THAT ARE ROUND

OUR FAVORITE FOOD GROUPS

Things You Need Math to Make

Buildings

Bridges

Computers

Calculators

Cars

Roads

W is for
"When are we ever gonna use this stuff, anyway?"

If you've ever asked that question while doing your math homework, this is for you.

When are you gonna use this stuff? At school, at home, at play, and at work. Any other questions?

You already use mathematical concepts every day whether you know it or not. Should you wear a raincoat to school today? You're using **probability.** Can you kick the ball into the goal, or should you pass? You're using geometry. If you're measuring the ingredients for a cake, you're using fractions. When you shop at the store, you make the smartest decisions if you understand both **quality** and **quantity** and the **units** used to measure what you're buying.

No matter what kind of job you get, chances are you will need math. Many jobs require some math, but by the time you graduate from college, *most* jobs will require *lots* of math.

You probably won't need to use an **abacus,** but mathematicians and computer scientists sometimes get ideas for entirely new ways of doing things by looking at old tools—like abacuses. **Binary** numbers are the basis for modern computers, so people who design new computers use the binary system. When chemists create new substances, they must understand the shapes of molecules, the kinds of **symmetry** they have, and how they fit together. Sometimes they want the molecules to **tessellate** and sometimes they do not. Chemists and all other scientists use **exponents** when they write big numbers—and often when they write small numbers, too.

Look at any man-made structure and you'll probably find **equilateral** triangles and **obtuse** angles (along with other kinds, of course). Geometry, the study of angles and shapes, is crucial to architecture, engineering, surveying, and navigation—not to mention art, photography, interior decoration, and billiards! Since **Fibonacci** numbers appear in some of the most surprising places, you may do a better job if you understand them, whether you're a landscaper, a painter, a musician, or a biologist.

Anyone who works with money must understand **hundreds,** but businesspeople, bankers, economists, and other money managers use a lot more math than that. They make graphs and read other people's graphs every day. If they don't know their x-axis from their **y-axis,** their graphs are going to look awfully funny. Doctors, too, must make and read graphs. They use **probability** in deciding on treatments and calculating dosages of medicine and other things.

Statements starting with **"if"** are important in an area of math called logic. Logic helps to solve problems and make sense out of confusing ideas. Lawyers use logical thinking to win cases in court. The math of topology—including the ideas behind **Möbius strips** and the **Königsberg** bridge problem—helps many kinds of workers, including those who lay electric cable, analyze DNA, or design circuits for computer chips.

Carpenters, surveyors, welders, painters, roofers, electricians, plumbers, auto mechanics, and many other kinds of workers use math on a daily basis. Their work involves measuring, calculating, and predicting in mathematical ways. If they don't do the math right, they will have some mighty unhappy customers. Imagine a house built without math. Would the walls meet in the right place? Would the roof keep you dry if no one knew how to measure the angles? Would there be enough paint to cover the walls? Would the electrical current be adequate to run a television and a toaster at the same time?

These examples all come from today's jobs. We don't know about tomorrow's jobs. Some of them haven't even been invented yet! But we know one thing about the best jobs of the future: they're gonna use math.

More math:

Tonight's dinner is an independent event, so the probability of being served broccoli is low. Hooray!

Games That Use Math

Mankala

Marbles

Tic Tac Toe

checkers

Card Games

...and W is also for

ware

weight

$2x = 4$

$\dfrac{24}{8} - x = 1$

$\dfrac{x}{16} = \dfrac{1}{8}$

$\sqrt{16} + x = 6$

$e = mx^2$

flour + water + x = pancakes

gopher − x = her

x marks the spot

X is for x

X is for x?

We can guess what you're saying. You're saying, "They're nuts." Or "They're bonkers." Or "They're cuckoo."

Well, that's the point. We don't know exactly what you're saying about us, so if we wanted to write your statement as a sentence, we'd have to write this:

They're _____.

Mathematicians like to write their sentences like this:

They = _____

It's called an *equation*. You can fill in the blank of this equation with "nuts" or "bonkers" or whatever you like.

One other thing. In math, we don't usually put blank lines in equations. Instead we use symbols. For example:

They = x

The x might be "nuts." It could also be "cuckoo." It could even be "wonderful" or "absolutely brilliant." No one knows for sure (except you), so x is called an *unknown*. It's also called a *variable*, because it changes, or varies. The x might be "nuts" in this equation and "awesome" in another equation, like this one:

My best friend = x

The math of unknowns is called *algebra*. (Be careful! In algebra, x does *not* mean "multiply.") X is not the only variable. You could just as well use y or z or n or anything else. The equations might be:

They = z or They = k or even They = ☺

But *x* seems to be the favorite variable. Here's why:

Reason = *x*

In other words, the reason is unknown.

In algebra, equations don't usually have words like "they" or "reason." Here's a more typical equation:

$$3 + 4 = x$$

In this equation, *x* can be only one thing, and you can easily figure out what it is. As soon as you figure it out, it won't be unknown. It's 7, of course. Here's another easy one.

$$12 - x = 10$$

In this equation, *x* is 2. The next equation is tougher because *x* shows up twice (and both *x*s have to be the same number because they're in the same equation).

$$24 \div x = 5 + x$$

Can you figure out what *x* equals? In other words, can you solve the equation? Try a few different numbers. We'll get you started. Try making *x* equal to 1. Stick a 1 into the equation wherever you see an *x*. Does that work? It says

$$24 \div 1 = 5 + 1$$

Is that true? Does 24 ÷ 1 equal 5 + 1? No. The two sides of the equation are not equal when *x* is 1. So make *x* another number, and another. Keep trying until you solve the equation.

Congratulations! You've begun doing algebra. Some day, when you've learned more algebra, you'll be able to solve equations in other quicker ways.

$$\frac{2 + x}{8} = 1$$

$$2 \times 2 \times 2 \times 2 \times 2 \times 2 = 2^x$$

2 wrongs ≠ 1 *x*

$$x^{100} = \text{one googol}$$

$$x^{\text{googol}} = \text{one googolplex}$$

if *x*, why z?

to *x*, or not to *x*, that is the question

a bird in the *x* = 2 in the bush

...and X is also for

x-axis

x-coordinate

Y is for y-axis

You've probably seen bar graphs like this one showing the favorite foods of everyone in Mr. Omnivore's class.

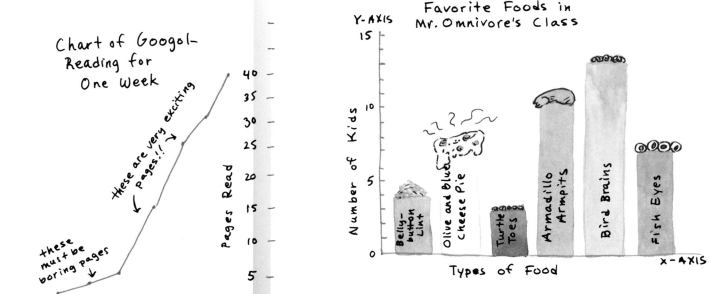

Chart of Googol-Reading for One Week

these are very exciting pages!! →

these must be boring pages ↓

Pages Read

40
35
30
25
20
15
10
5

X-AXIS   1   2   3   4   5   6   7

Days it Takes to Read Pages

Favorite Foods in Mr. Omnivore's Class

Y-AXIS 15

Number of Kids
10
5
0

Belly-button Lint — Olive and Blue Cheese Pie — Turtle Toes — Armadillo Armpits — Bird Brains — Fish Eyes

Types of Food

X-AXIS

If you want to know how many kids like each kind of food, trace your finger from the top of any bar to the vertical line on the left and read the number where your finger hits the line. That line is called the *y-axis*, or *vertical axis*. There is also a line at the bottom of the graph called the *x-axis*, or *horizontal axis*.

Here's another kind of graph, called a *line graph*. This one shows how far a tortoise has travelled in a one-hour race. A line graph also has a y-axis and an x-axis. The y-axis shows the distance in meters, and the x-axis shows the time. The race starts at 1:00 P.M. To see how far the tortoise has gone by 1:10, find 1:10 on the x-axis. Go straight up to the dot on the line, then move to the left until you reach the y-axis.

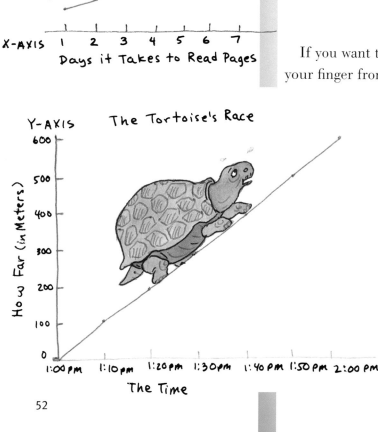

The Tortoise's Race

Y-AXIS
600
500
400
300
200
100
0

How Far (in Meters)

1:00 PM   1:10 PM   1:20 PM   1:30 PM   1:40 PM   1:50 PM   2:00 PM

The Time

You can see that the turtle has gone 100 meters. By 1:20, the tortoise has covered 200 meters. And so on. At the end of the one-hour race, the tortoise has gone 600 meters.

Here's another graph. It's similar, but it shows the hare's race instead of the tortoise's. The hare speeds right along, covering 500 meters in just 20 minutes. But then what happens?

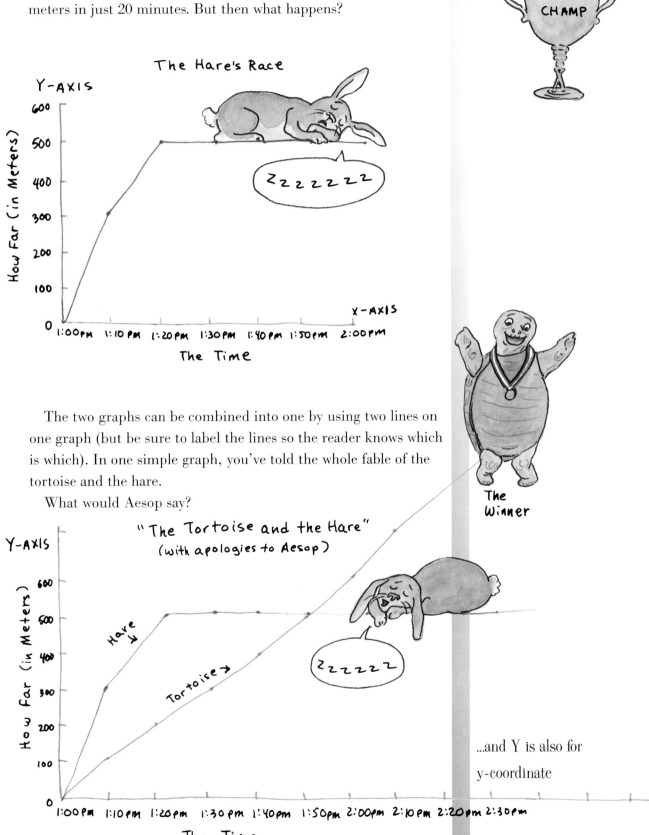

The two graphs can be combined into one by using two lines on one graph (but be sure to label the lines so the reader knows which is which). In one simple graph, you've told the whole fable of the tortoise and the hare.

What would Aesop say?

...and Y is also for y-coordinate

Z is for Zillion

No question about it, a *zillion* is "a lot." But it doesn't mean any particular amount, so it's not a number. A number is a certain amount. Three is a number and three hundred is a number. One million is a number and two billion is a number. So are a trillion, a quadrillion, a quintillion, a sextillion, a septillion, an octillion, a nonillion and a decillion. And a googol and a googolplex. If you had enough time (and nothing better to do), you could count to any of these numbers. But you could never count to a zillion because you wouldn't know when you got there. It's not a number.

There are other words like zillion. They're fun to say, and they all mean "a lot":

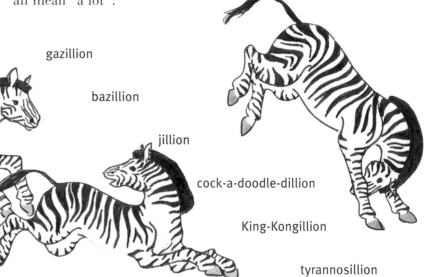

gazillion

bazillion

jillion

cock-a-doodle-dillion

King-Kongillion

tyrannosillion

You can make up your own words...   Awesomillion!

...and Z is also for

zero

54

Glossary

ACUTE An angle smaller than a right angle (less than 90°). [See O is for Obtuse]

ALGEBRA A branch of mathematics that uses unknown quantities (variables) that are usually represented by letters. [See X is for *x*]

ANGLE The shape formed where two lines meet. [See O is for Obtuse]

ARC Part of the circumference of a circle or part of a curve.

ARCHITECTURE The art and science of designing buildings.

AREA The size of a surface, measured in square units, such as square centimeters, square inches, square meters, acres, etc.

ASYMMETRY Lacking symmetry. If an object has no symmetry, it is said to be "asymmetrical." [See S is for Symmetry]

AVERAGE The middle, or "typical" value when there are several numbers. Averages are a simple way to get a general view of a group. There are three kinds of averages: mean, median, and mode.

AXIS 1) A line around which an object spins. 2) A line at the side or bottom of a graph.

BAR GRAPH A way of showing numerical information as a series of bars of different lengths. [See P is for Probability and Y is for y-axis]

BASE In every number system, each place value can be filled by a certain number of digits. That number is the "base" of the system. Our number system is Base 10 (the decimal system) because each place value can be 0, 1, 2, 3, 4, 5, 6, 7, 8 or 9: ten possibilities in all. [For Base 2, see B is for Binary]

BASE NUMBER When numbers are expressed with exponents, the number written at the bottom (to show that it is being multiplied by itself a certain number of times) is called the base number. [See E is for Exponent]

BISECT To divide an angle in half.

CATENARY CURVE If you hang a chain from two points, it makes a curve called a catenary curve. If you hang weights from it at equal intervals, it changes slightly to become a parabola, or parabolic curve. The main cables (called catenary cables) of a suspension bridge like the Golden Gate Bridge make this curve until vertical suspenders are added, at which time the cables make a parabolic curve.

CHAOS To most people, chaos means a state of confusion. To scientists and mathematicians it means a system (a set of causes and effects) that acts in ways that are very hard to predict because very slight changes result in large effects. Weather is considered a chaotic system.

CHART A visual presentation of information, often in rows and columns, making it easy to compare items (like prices or populations) or see equivalences (like conversions from miles to kilometers).

CIRCLE All the points that are the same distance from a fixed point. The fixed point is the center of the circle, and the distance is called the radius. Since an infinite number of points are the same distance from a fixed point, they "run together" and make a curve. This curve is closed and it has an infinite number of lines of symmetry. [See Curve and S is for Symmetry]

CIRCUMFERENCE The distance around a circle. The word *circumference* can also mean the outside edge of the circle itself, as contrasted with its total area.

COORDINATE One of a pair of numbers that tells you where a point on a graph is located, relative to its horizontal axis and vertical axis (usually called x-axis and y-axis, respectively). For example, the point specified as (3,5) is a point that is three units along the x-axis and 5 units along the y-axis. [See Y is for y-axis]

CUBE 1) A three-dimensional shape with six faces, all of them squares. 2) When a number (let's say 2, but it could be any number) is multiplied by itself three times (2 X 2 X 2), the result (8) is called its cube. It can also be written with an exponent as 2^3.

CUBE ROOT The number that has been multiplied by itself three times to get another number. Since 8 is the cube of 2, we say that 2 is the cube root of 8.

CURVE The route of a point that has moved in a continuous bend. If it ends up where it started, the curve is called a "closed curve"; if it ends up somewhere else, it is an "open curve."

CYLINDER Take two identical circles and connect them with a curved surface to make a solid shape like a soup can. Voilà! You've got a cylinder. (Cylinders can also be made by connecting two ellipses in the same way.)

DATA Collected information is called data. Often the information is numerical. The singular of "data" is "datum." So you can never have one data. If you've just got one, it's a datum!

DECIMAL POINT A point placed in a number. All the digits to the right of the decimal point have a value less than one.

DECIMAL SYSTEM The number system we use, also known as Base 10 (see base) or the denary system. In the decimal counting system, each place value can be filled with any one of ten numbers, and each place has a value 10 times greater than the one to its right (the ones place, the tens place, the hundreds place, etc.).

DEGREE 1) A measurement of temperature. 2) A unit of measurement for angles.

DENOMINATOR See fraction.

DENSITY A way of comparing weight to volume. Which weighs more, a pound of bricks or a pound of cotton? They both weigh the same: one pound! But which weighs more, a bushel of bricks or a bushel of cotton? The bricks weigh a lot more. We say bricks have a higher density than cotton because their weight per volume is higher.

DIAMETER The distance across a circle, through the center, from one point on the circumference to another. Or the line segment that passes through the center of a circle from one side of the circumference to another.

DODECAHEDRON A polyhedron of 12 faces, which are all regular pentagons.

ELLIPSE If you "stretch out" a circle, you'll get an ellipse. Ellipses have only two lines of symmetry.

EQUATION A mathematical statement of two things being equal (separated by an = sign).

EQUIVALENT FRACTIONS Fractions that have the same value even though they are expressed with different numerators and denominators. For example, $\frac{1}{2}$ and $\frac{2}{4}$ are equivalent fractions.

ESTIMATE An educated guess that gives a rough idea of an answer or a measurement.

FACE The flat side of a polyhedron. The line where two faces meet each other is called an edge. The point where three or more faces meet is called a vertex.

FACTORS A whole number that can divide into another number exactly. For example, the factors of 10 are 1, 2, 5, and 10. There are more factors of 12: They are 1, 2, 3, 4, 6, and 12.

FORMULA A mathematical rule that answers a particular question. For example, the formula for the area of a rectangle is the length multiplied by the width. [For another example, see Euler's formula in R is for Rhombicosidodecahedron.]

FRACTION A part of a whole, shown as two numbers separated by a line. The bottom number, or denominator, tells how many parts the whole has been divided into. The top number, or numerator, shows how many of these parts are included in the fraction. In the fraction $\frac{3}{8}$, for example, the whole is divided into 8 parts (the denominator), but only 3 of them are included in this fraction (the numerator).

GEOMETRY The study of space, including points, lines, angles, and shapes.

GIGA- As a prefix, "giga-" means one billion (1,000,000,000). One gigabyte is 1,000,000,000 bytes.

GOLDEN SECTION (also called GOLDEN RATIO or MEAN) Imagine a line divided into two sections so that the ratio of the whole line to the larger section is the same as the ratio of the larger section to the smaller section. The ratio turns out to be about 1.618. This ratio is found in nature, art, and architecture. It is found in the proportions of the Parthenon and the Great Pyramid at Giza, and in paintings by Leonardo da Vinci and Michelangelo. The ratio of consecutive Fibonacci numbers approaches the Golden Section as the Fibonacci numbers get bigger. [See F is for Fibonacci and N is for Nature]

GRAM A measurement of mass in the metric system, or Système Internationale (SI). One thousand grams is a kilogram. There are 454 grams in a pound.

GRAPH A visual display of numerical data, usually showing the data in relation to horizontal and vertical axes (x- and y-axes, respectively). [See Y is for y-axis]

HELIX A three-dimensional spiral that winds around a line (or "axis").

HORSEPOWER A unit for measuring power, usually applied to engines. One horsepower equals 550 foot-pounds per second. It's based on the power of one horse.

HYPOTENEUSE In a right triangle, the hypoteneuse is the side opposite the right angle. It is the longest side of the triangle.

INFINITE Greater than any number or size or quantity. Endless or immeasurably large. "Infinity" is the state of being infinite in space, time, or number. Contrary to popular belief, "infinity" is not the "largest number in the world" because it is not a number.

INFINITESSIMAL Smaller than any number or quantity, except for zero. Immeasurably small.

INTEGER A whole number like 0, 1, 2, 3, 793, 1,000,000, or similar negative numbers. Fractions like $\frac{1}{2}$ or $\frac{3}{8}$ or $\frac{139}{1100}$ are not integers.

INTERSECTION 1) The place where two lines (or surfaces) cross each other. 2) A set that contains the items shared by several other sets, but no items that are contained in only one (or none) of those sets. [See V is for Venn Diagram]

IRRATIONAL NUMBER A number that cannot be expressed either as an integer or a fraction. Some examples are $\sqrt{2}$, π, and the golden section.

ISOSCELES TRIANGLE A triangle with two equal sides.

JORDAN CURVE A curve that doesn't cross itself anywhere and stays in one plane (is two-dimensional). Also called a simple closed curve.

KLEIN BOTTLE A bottle with only one surface—an outside but no inside! Think of it as a three-dimensional version of a Möbius strip, and in fact, if you could cut a Klein bottle in half it would become two Möbius strips. Unlike the Möbius strip, a Klein bottle cannot exist except in the imagination of topologists!

LATITUDE Distance north or south of the Equator, measured in degrees. (The Equator is defined as 0° and the North and South Poles as 90° North and 90° South.) A degree of latitude is about 69 miles. Latitude and longitude are used in navigation and global positioning.

LINE GRAPH A kind of graph where data is shown as a line or curve. The data may originally be plotted as individual points (or dots), but the points are later connected by a line, and sometimes they are replaced by the line.

LOCUS A set of points that all have a certain quality. The locus of points that are all 3 centimeters from another point on a piece of paper would be a circle. The circle would have a 3-centimeter radius and a 6-centimeter diameter.

LOGIC The branch of math that has to do with reasoning and proof.

LONGITUDE Distance east or west on the surface of the Earth, measured in degrees. Imaginary lines of longitude, called "meridians," run from the North to the South poles. In diagrams, they make the Earth look like it's divided into wedges, like the sections of an orange.

MANKALA (Also MANCALA) A group of games involving mathematical thinking that come from Africa and parts of Asia. Oware (or ware) is a mankala game played in West Africa with a two-row board and beans as counters. [See W is for When...]

MASS The quantity of matter that an object contains. No matter how strong the gravitational force exerted on an object, its mass remains the same, but its weight changes. If you go to Jupiter, your mass will stay the same, but your weight will greatly increase. (Don't go if you're trying to lose weight!) People often say "weight" when they mean mass. Pounds and grams are actually measurements of mass.

MEAN One of the three kinds of averages. To get the mean, add all the quantities you have and divide that sum by the number of quantities you added. The mean of 1, 3, and 8 is 4.

MEDIAN Another one of the three kinds of averages. The median is the number in the middle. If you have a set of numbers, look for the one that is smaller than and larger than an equal number of other values. That's the median. The median of 3, 6, 7, 9, and 11 is 7.

METRIC SYSTEM The system of measurements used in almost every country of the world, except the United States. It is based on meters as the basic unit of length and grams as the basic unit of mass, along with other units for other types of measurements, such as liters for volume. In the metric system, most units are multiples of each other by factors of 10, 100, or 1,000. Metric units are also known as SI units.

MODE The last of the three kinds of averages. It's the number that occurs the most frequently in a set of numbers. The mode of 1, 2, 5, 5, 5, 9, 10, 11, 11, 14, and 15 is 5. The median is 9, and the mean is 8.

NEGATIVE NUMBER A number less than zero, such as −1, −2, −3, and so forth. It is easy to understand in terms of money. If you have exactly $10, you could say you have +10 dollars. But instead, if you owe someone $10, you could say you have −10 dollars. Then if someone gave you $10, you would have $0.

NIM An ancient mathematical game where 20 counters are laid out (you can use coins) and the two players take turns picking up one, two, or three counters at a time. The player who picks up the last counter loses. You can invent your own variations and try to figure out a strategy to win.

NUMERATOR See fraction.

OCTAVE In music, one note is an octave higher than another if its sound has twice as many vibrations per second as the lower one. On the musical scale, these two notes are eight notes apart.

OWARE See Mankala.

PALINDROME A number (or word or sentence) that is the same frontwards or backwards. The numbers 292 and 3,008,003 are palindromes. The years 1991 and 2002 are palindromes.

PARABOLA A kind of U-shaped curve where parallel lines reflect to one point, called the focus. Parabolas are useful in many ways. Satellite dishes have a parabolic shape, and so do car headlights. (In headlights, the light leaves the focus, reflects off the inside of the parabola, and leaves the lamp in parallel beams.)

PARALLEL Lines that stay the same distance apart for their entire length. If you could extend them infinitely, they would never meet.

PARALLELOGRAM A four-sided shape with opposite sides that are parallel and of equal length. Opposite angles are also equal.

PERCENT A way of showing amounts as a part of a hundred. Fifty percent (50%) means 50 parts out of 100, which is also one-half. Ninety-nine percent means 99 parts of a hundred. Four parts out of five is 80 percent because $\frac{4}{5}$ is equivalent to $\frac{80}{100}$.

PI The ratio of the circumference of a circle to its diameter, commonly shown by the Greek letter π. In other words, if you measured the distance around a circle exactly and divided it by the distance across the circle, you would get π as your answer. In the decimal system, it is about 3.142, but not exactly. It cannot be expressed exactly as a decimal number because it is an irrational number.

PIE CHART A way to show data where a circle is divided into wedges (resembling slices of pie) to show different quantities.

POINT A single location with no dimensions—infinitesimally small.

POLYGON A closed, flat shape with straight sides. The smallest possible number of sides is 3. There is no largest possible number, but as the number of sides gets larger and larger, the shape looks more and more like a circle. If you could have a polygon with an infinite number of sides, it would be a circle. But you can't!

POLYHEDRON A solid shape. Its surface is made of four or more faces. [See R is for Rhombicosidodecahedron]

PRIME NUMBER A number that can be divided evenly by 1 and itself, and nothing else. Some prime numbers are 2, 3, 5, 7, 11, 13, 17... (1 is not considered a prime number.) No even numbers are primes because they are all divisible by 2.

PROPORTION See ratio.

PYTHAGOREAN THEOREM Pythagoras, an ancient Greek philosopher and mathematician, discovered something very important about right triangles. If you square (multiply by itself) each of the two sides that are next to the right angle, and add them together, the sum will equal the square of the hypotenuse. If the sides are called "a" and "b" and the hypotenuse is called "c," the Pythagorean theorem can be written as an equation: $a^2 + b^2 = c^2$. It is one of the most famous equations in all of mathematics.

QUADRILATERAL A four-sided polygon.

QUIPU In the Inca empire of South America (about 1400–1540 C.E.), the government kept track of the numbers of people, products, taxes, etc., on sets of strings called quipus (KEE-poos). Each quipu had several strings of different colors, and knots on the strings indicated different quantities.

RADIUS The distance from the center of a circle to the circumference. Also can refer to a line segment that goes from the center to the circumference.

RATIO A way of comparing numbers. If the number 1 is being compared to the number 5, the ratio of those two numbers can be shown as 1:5 or $\frac{1}{5}$. We say that any other two numbers in which the second number is 5 times bigger than the first (like 2 and 10) have the same ratio, or proportion, as 1 and 5. So, the ratio 2:10 is equivalent to the ratio 1:5 (just as the fraction $\frac{2}{10}$ is equivalent to $\frac{1}{5}$).

RHOMBUS A parallelogram that has all four sides of equal length. [See D is for Diamond]

RIGHT ANGLE An angle that measures exactly 90°. Four of them together would be 360°, which is a complete circle, so a right angle is often thought of as one-quarter of a circle. [See O is for Obtuse]

RIGHT TRIANGLE A triangle with one right angle.

ROTATIONAL SYMMETRY [See S is for Symmetry]

SCALENE A triangle with no two sides of the same length.

SEQUENCE A list of numbers that follows a pattern. Try to find the patterns in these four sequences: [1, 2, 3, 4, 5...] [2, 4, 6, 8, 10...] [1, 2, 4, 8, 16, 32...] [1, 4, 9, 16, 25, 36...]

SET A collection of numbers or objects that have certain properties that distinguish them from numbers or objects that don't have those properties. [See V is for Venn Diagram]

SI UNIT See metric system.

SPHERE A round, solid shape. Balls are spheres. Mathematically, a sphere is defined as the three-dimensional shape whose surface is the locus of points that are the same distance from a single point.

SPIRAL An open-ended curve. It can be two-dimensional or three-dimensional and it can wind around a point or a line (axis). [See N is for Nature]

SQUARE 1) A rectangle with all four sides of equal length. 2) When a number is multiplied by itself, the result is called a square, or square number. The square of 12 is 144 because 12 X 12 = 144.

SQUARE ROOT A number that has been multiplied by itself to produce a square. The square root of 4 is 2, and the square root of 144 is 12.

TABLE In math, a table is a way of arranging information (usually numbers) in rows and columns so different items can be compared, and associations can be seen.

TANGRAM A Chinese puzzle made of a square cut into seven pieces.

TOPOLOGY The study of what happens to objects when they are stretched, shrunk, cut, turned inside-out, or distorted in other ways. Topologists want to know what changes (and how an object changes), and what stays the same. [See Klein bottle and M is for Möbius Strip]

TRIANGLE A three-sided polygon. The sum of all the internal angles of a triangle is always 180°.

TRISKAIDEKAPHOBIA Fear of the number 13. (No joke! Would fear of the number 100 be "centiphobia"?)

UNION A set that contains all the items that belong to either or both of two sets. If Set A contains {1, 3, 5, 7, 9} and Set B contains {1, 4, 9, 16, 25} the union of Sets A and B is {1, 3, 4, 5, 7, 9, 16, 25}. The union of more than two sets contains all the items that belong to any of those sets. [See Venn is for Venn Diagram]

VARIABLE To solve problems, mathematicians often use letters to represent the numbers that they wish to find. The letters are called "unknowns" or "variables." *X* is the most common variable, but other letters (or symbols) also work. Sometimes two or more variables are used on one equation, such as $a^2 + b^2 = c^2$ (the Pythagorean theorem). [See X is for *x*]

VERTEX On a flat shape, the point where two or more lines meet is the vertex. On a solid shape, the pont where three or more faces meet is also called a vertex. (The plural of vertex is "vertices.") Euler's formula (v + s = e + 2) lets you know how many vertices are in a polyhedron if you know how many sides and edges it has. [See R is for Rhombicosidodecahedron]

VOLUME A measurement of the space contained by a solid shape.

WARE See Mankala.

WEIGHT The force pulling an object down toward the Earth (or other body.) See also mass.

X-AXIS The horizontal axis in a graph. [See Y is for y-axis]

X-COORDINATE The number that gives the location of a point along the x-axis of a graph.

Y-COORDINATE The number that gives the location of a point along the y-axis of a graph. [See Y is for y-axis]

ZERO The number that means nothing actually means a great deal. For centuries, scholars argued over whether it was a number. Leonardo of Pisa, or Fibonacci, solved the problem by saying it is a number with meaning, and it can be used as a "place holder" or a position on a scale.